Cuisine PERNOD®

Mary Cadogan

PHOTOGRAPHS : JAMES MURPHY

FOREWORD BY

Anton Edelmann

Produced for Campbell Distillers Limited by Good Books
(GB Publications Limited),
Lagard Farm, Whitley, Wilts SN12 8RL

Copyright © Campbell Distillers Limited 1990

ISBN 0 946555 13 3

Editor: Helen Slater
Design: Wendy Bann
Cover design: Les Dominey
Illustrations: Diana Leadbetter
Stylist: Sarah Wiley ·

Typesetting by Wyvern Typesetting Ltd, Bristol
Colour Separation by Fotographics Ltd, London and Hong Kong
Printed in Great Britain by Hazell, Watson and Viney Ltd, Aylesbury

For any further information about Pernod, contact

UK:
Campbell Distillers Limited, Pernod House
924 Great West Road, Brentford, Middlesex TW8 9DY

Australia:
Orlando Wines & Spirits Pty Limited
284 Carrington Street
Adelaide
South Australia 5000

Holland:
Koninklijke Cooymans BV
Branderijstraat 1
5223 AS Postous 416
5201 AK's Hertogenbosch

USA:
Austin Nichols & Company Incorporated
156 East 46th Street
New York
NY 10017

Contents

Foreword

Anton Edelmann is a chef of international renown, having worked in Brussels, Paris, Geneva and Düsseldorf before coming to London. He has won a number of major awards and prizes, and has himself been a judge at several international competitions. He has been Maître Chef des Cuisines at The Savoy since 1982. His kitchen there, with a staff of 100, is one of the busiest and most creative in London.

For those who know Pernod only as a drink, it will come as a surprise to learn that it can be an intriguing and taste-enhancing ingredient in cooking. Over the years, many international chefs have used Pernod with fish to delicious effect.

You will see from the recipes in this book that Pernod lends itself equally to a variety of meat and poultry dishes and desserts.

Sauces, soups, pâtés, kebabs, sorbets, parfaits, even salads and snacks, can also be transformed by the imaginative culinary addition of this 'taste of France'.

What gives Pernod its distinctive flavour and aroma is the unique combination of herbs and plants it contains – things like anise, fennel, chamomile and coriander, which stimulate the appetite as well as the palate.

So, raise your glass of Pernod to salute this book of recipes.

Bon appétit!

Anton Edelmann
Maître Chef des Cuisines
The Savoy, London

The History of Pernod

In 1790, the second year of the French Revolution, a certain Doctor Pierre Ordinaire was fleeing France in fear for his life. As a supporter of the king, he was a prime candidate for Madame Guillotine.

Dr Ordinaire settled in Couvet, Switzerland, where he continued to practice medicine, which at that time included the preparation of herbal elixirs. By 1792, he had created a potent combination of fifteen medicinal herbs steeped in alcohol. The ingredients included anise étoile (star anise), fennel, common balm, parsley, chamomile, coriander, veronica, spinach and wormwood. He named his concoction 'absinthe', a word derived from *Artemisia absinthium*, the botanical name of wormwood.

A short time later, Dr Ordinaire died, but not before passing his secret recipe on to his housekeeper and assistant, Madame Henriot. She opened a small shop where she sold absinthe as a *digestif*. An enterprising Frenchman named Major Henri Dubied was a regular customer at her shop. So convinced was he of the benefits of absinthe that in 1797 he bought the recipe from Mme Henriot, and went into partnership with his son-in-law, Henri-Louis Pernod. That same year they opened their first factory in Switzerland, to be followed eight years later by a bigger factory across the border in the French town of Pontarlier. By then the product had become known as Pernod, to distinguish it from the imitators that had already appeared.

The popularity of Pernod grew steadily, helped by the fact that for a while it was issued as part of the French Army's daily rations, and also through its enthusiastic adoption by the artistic milieu in *fin de siècle* Paris. From there the taste for anise spread through the whole of French society.

By 1915, however, it was realised that the wormwood in Pernod was causing illness in some drinkers, and its use was prohibited by law. At the same time, the alcoholic strength of Pernod was reduced, resulting in the drink as we know it today.

In the ultra-modern 'Pernoderie' factory at Creteil on the outskirts of Paris, Pernod is still made to the same secret recipe, using the latest electronic techniques to ensure the product is perfect. A highly-concentrated essence is distilled from anise étoile or fennel. A further fourteen herbs are macerated in rectified alcohol, and then distilled into an aromatic extract. The skilful blending of this aniseed essence and herbal extract produces the unique Pernod flavour – something which has delighted discerning drinkers for almost two hundred years.

Above: King prawns with Pernod mayonnaise (p.1)   *Below*: Poached scallops with fromage frais (p.2)

Soups and Starters

King Prawns with Pernod Mayonnaise

Preparation time: 25 minutes, plus chilling time
Cooking time: 8–10 minutes

This dish is ideal for entertaining as the mayonnaise can be made several hours in advance, leaving only the prawns to cook before serving.

16 headless king prawns, uncooked
1 teaspoon paprika
½ teaspoon salt
2 tablespoons lemon juice
2 teaspoons Pernod
2 tablespoons sunflower oil
lemon wedges, to serve

Pernod Mayonnaise
2 egg yolks

pinch cayenne
½ pint (300ml) olive oil
1 tablespoon snipped chives
1 small pickled gherkin, chopped
1 teaspoon capers
1 tablespoon lemon juice
1 teaspoon Pernod
a pinch of salt
1–2 teaspoons boiling water

1. Peel the prawns, leaving the tail section on. Cut each down the back and remove the black intestine. Rinse and dry the prawns. Mix together the paprika, salt, lemon juice and Pernod and stir in the prawns. Chill for 30 minutes.
2. Place the egg yolks in a bowl with the cayenne and beat lightly together. Beating all the time, add the olive oil drop by drop, until a thick shiny sauce is formed. This can be done in a food processor or liquidiser, but always add the oil as slowly as possible.
3. Stir in the chives, gherkins, capers, lemon juice, Pernod and salt. Add a little boiling water if the sauce is too thick.
4. Heat the sunflower oil in a frying pan, add the prawns and fry until pink all over and cooked through (about 8–10 minutes). Serve warm with the Pernod mayonnaise and wedges of lemon.

Serves 4

When doubling the amounts in a recipe, only increase the measure of salt by one and a half times.

Poached Scallops with Fromage Frais

Preparation time: 15 minutes   Cooking time: 10–12 minutes

Serve as a starter for four or a light meal for two.

A potted basil plant on a warm window sill in the kitchen will provide fresh leaves throughout the seasons. Tear the leaves rather than chop them to preserve their subtle flavour. Pinch out the growing tips to encourage the plant to bush out with extra leaves.

3 ripe tomatoes
8 scallops
1 shallot, chopped finely
¼ pint (150ml) dry white wine
1 tablespoon Pernod

8 basil leaves, torn into pieces
3 tablespoons fromage frais
salt and pepper
basil leaves, to garnish

1. Skin, seed and chop the tomatoes finely. Rinse and dry the scallops. Carefully remove the orange coral, then slice each white piece across into three rounds.
2. In a small, shallow pan, heat the shallots, wine and Pernod. Simmer for 2 minutes, then add the scallops and corals and poach very gently for 2 minutes. Remove with a slotted spoon and keep warm.
3. Increase the heat under the poaching liquid and boil until reduced by half. Reduce the heat to a gentle simmer and stir in the tomatoes, basil leaves and fromage frais. Heat through gently, then taste and add salt and pepper.
4. Spoon the sauce onto warmed plates and arrange the scallops on top. Garnish with a basil leaf and serve.

Serves 2 or 4

Chilled Cucumber Soup

Preparation time: 20 minutes, plus chilling time
Cooking time: 15 minutes

This is a light and refreshing soup, ideal for serving outdoors on a summer's day.

1 bunch spring onions
1 large cucumber
2 tablespoons sunflower oil
1 tablespoon plain flour
1 pint (600ml) vegetable stock

salt and pepper
1 tablespoon Pernod
¼ pint (150ml) plain yogurt
cucumber slices, to garnish

Use a balloon whisk to get rid of stray lumps in sauces or soups.

1. Trim and finely chop the spring onions. Peel and chop the cucumber. Heat the oil in a frying pan, add the onion and cucumber and cook until the onions are tender (about 5 minutes). Stir in the flour and cook for 1 minute.
2. Gradually add the stock and bring to the boil, stirring all the time until

the sauce thickens. Add the salt, pepper and Pernod, cover and simmer for 5 minutes, stirring occasionally.

3. Remove from the heat and allow to cool. When the mixture is cool, purée it, a little at a time, in a blender or food processor. Stir in the yogurt and chill until required. To serve, pour the soup into four bowls and float a few thin cucumber slices on top.

Serves 4

Chilled Melon with Mint

Preparation time: 15 minutes, plus chilling time

An ideal starter before a rich meal of game or red meat.

1 Charantais melon
1 Ogen Melon
1 tablespoon Pernod

3 tablespoons fresh orange juice
2 teaspoons chopped mint
sprigs of mint, to garnish

Test the ripeness of an Ogen or Charantais melon by gently pressing the stalk end of the fruit. When ripe, it will yield slightly.

1. Cut the melons in half and remove the seeds. Scoop out the flesh with a melon baller, or peel the melons and cut the flesh into cubes. Place the melon in a bowl.
2. Mix together the Pernod, orange juice and mint and pour over the melon. Mix together gently. Chill for 1–2 hours, then divide the melon between four glass dishes. Garnish with sprigs of mint.

Serves 4

Chilled dishes containing melons benefit from being removed from the refrigerator at least 30 minutes before serving, as when the fruit is too cold it loses flavour.

Tuna and Fennel Salad

Preparation time: 20 minutes

Serve this country-style starter with warm crusty bread.

7oz (200g) can tuna, drained
14oz (400g) can borlotti or red
*   kidney beans, drained*
4oz (125g) black olives, pitted
1 fennel bulb
6 spring onions, chopped finely

Dressing
4 tablespoons mayonnaise
2 teaspoons Pernod
1 teaspoon Dijon mustard
1 teaspoon wine vinegar
1 tablespoon olive oil
salt and pepper

Fennel is commonly associated with fish dishes, but is also good with pork, in soups, sauces and salads. Both its green, feathery leaves and aromatic seeds can be used.

1. Break up the tuna into chunks and mix with the beans and olives. Cut the fennel into quarters, remove the tough root and slice the fennel very thinly. Add the spring onions to the tuna with the fennel. Stir well, then transfer to four salad bowls.
2. Place all the dressing ingredients in a bowl and whisk well until smooth. Spoon a little dressing onto each salad and serve.

Serves 4

Chicken Liver and Mushroom Pâté

Preparation time: 20 minutes, plus chilling time
Cooking time: 10 minutes

This inexpensive pâté will keep for up to 4 days in the fridge.

8oz (250g) chicken livers
3oz (75g) unsalted butter
2 cloves garlic, crushed
4oz (125g) cup mushrooms,
   chopped
1 teaspoon mustard
1 teaspoon Pernod

2 teaspoons chopped parsley
2 teaspoons snipped chives
salt and pepper
1 bay leaf
pink or black peppercorns
toasted French bread
1 bunch radishes

Fresh herbs can be frozen for winter use. Either place in bunches in a rigid container, then crumble when frozen, or chop finely and freeze with a little water in ice cube trays.

1. Rinse and dry the chicken livers, removing any dark patches. Melt half the butter in a frying pan, add the garlic and fry for 1 minute. Add the chicken livers and fry gently for 3–4 minutes, stirring all the time. Add the mushrooms, and cook for a further 3 minutes.
2. Stir in the mustard, Pernod, parsley, chives, salt and pepper and bring to the boil. Cook for 2 minutes, then transfer the mixture to a liquidiser or food processor and blend until smooth.
3. Turn the pâté into a small dish and smooth the top with the back of a spoon. Gently heat the remaining butter and pour carefully over the pâté to seal it completely. Arrange the bay leaf and peppercorns on top. When the pâté is cool, place it in the fridge to set completely. Serve with slices of toasted French bread and radishes.

Serves 4

Warm Duck Breast Salad

Preparation time: 15 minutes   Cooking time: 20 minutes

With this Chinese method of roasting, the meat stays deliciously moist and the skin becomes crisp and glazed.

1 tablespoon Pernod
1 tablespoon soy sauce
2 teaspoons clear honey
2 boneless duck breasts
¼ pint (150ml) boiling water
4 tablespoons double cream
1 tablespoon hazelnut oil

2 teaspoons fresh lime juice
salt and pepper
4 radicchio leaves
1 small red onion, sliced thinly
curly endive
chervil
4 wedges of lime

1. Make a glaze by mixing together the Pernod, soy sauce and honey in a small bowl. Brush this over the duck breasts. Place the duck on a rack

Above: Chicken liver and mushroom pâté (p.4)   *Below*: Warm duck breast salad (p.4)

Above: Wild mushroom salad (p.8)   *Below*: Mussels with creamy fennel sauce (p.7)

over a shallow ovenproof dish. Pour the boiling water into the dish. Roast the duck at 180°C (350°F/Gas Mark 4) for 20–25 minutes, brushing the skin once with the glaze. Keep the duck warm while preparing the sauce.

2. Transfer the juices in the dish to a food processor or liquidiser. Add the cream, oil and lime juice and blend well. Taste and add salt and pepper if necessary.
3. Place a radicchio leaf on each serving plate and fill with sliced onion, curly endive and chervil. Slice the duck thinly and arrange the slices on the plates. Pour the sauce over the duck and garnish with lime.

Serves 4

To substitute yogurt for cream, stabilize it first by mixing 1 teaspoon of cornflour with a little cold water, stir into a small carton of yogurt and cook gently for 10 minutes, stirring constantly. This prevents it from separating in cooking.

Mussels with Creamy Fennel Sauce

Preparation time: 25 minutes   Cooking time: 15–20 minutes

When they are available, try using clams instead of mussels.

3lb (1.5kg) mussels in shells
1oz (25g) butter
1 onion, chopped
1 fennel bulb, chopped
2 tablespoons Pernod

1 egg yolk
¼ pint (150ml) double cream
1 teaspoon chopped tarragon
1 teaspoon lemon juice
salt and pepper

1. Wash the mussels in several changes of cold water, then scrub the shells well, and remove the beard between the shells. Discard any open mussels that do not close when tapped sharply.
2. Heat the butter in a large saucepan, add the onion and fennel and fry for 5 minutes, until softened. Add the Pernod and mussels, cover and cook over a high heat, shaking the pan until all the mussels have opened (about 5 minutes).
3. Pour the mussels into a strainer, catching the cooking liquid in a bowl underneath. Transfer the liquid to a saucepan and boil to reduce by half. Remove one shell from each mussel and place the mussels in shells on four warmed serving dishes. Keep warm.
4. Beat together the egg yolk and cream, remove the cooking liquid from heat and stir in the cream mixture. Add tarragon, lemon juice, salt and pepper and reheat gently, stirring all the time, being careful not to let the sauce boil. When the sauce is slightly thickened and glossy, pour it over the mussels and serve.

Mussels are in season in the autumn and winter. The shells must be tightly closed when purchased, and discard any that are open. **Always** eat mussels on the day that you buy them.

Serves 4

Wild Mushroom Salad

Brown cap mushrooms, chanterelles and oyster mushrooms are particularly suitable, but button mushrooms can be used instead.

2oz (50g) streaky bacon
2 slices day-old bread
3 tablespoons olive oil
selection of salad leaves (i.e. green
    batavia, curly endive, roquette,
    oak leaf lettuce)
4–6oz (125g–175g) wild mushrooms

Dressing
1 tablespoon red wine vinegar
½ teaspoon Dijon mustard
pinch sugar
4 tablespoons olive oil
1 teaspoon Pernod
salt and pepper

Add a teaspoon of Pernod to your usual salad dressing for a subtle herby taste. A touch of honey will bring out the flavours.

1. Remove the rind from the bacon. Fry the bacon in its own fat until crisp, then drain on kitchen paper and cut into small pieces. Cut the bread into small cubes. Heat the oil in the frying pan, add the bread and fry until crisp and golden brown. Drain on kitchen paper.
2. Divide the washed and dried salad leaves between four individual bowls and sprinkle with the bacon and croutons. Wipe the mushrooms and halve if necessary. Scatter them over the salads.
3. Place the dressing ingredients in a screw-topped jar and shake well until slightly thickened. Just before serving, pour the dressing over the salads.

Serves 4

Asparagus with Woodman's Sauce

An elegant starter for a special dinner. The sauce can be kept warm for up to 30 minutes in a bowl over hot (but not boiling) water.

Chop herbs in a glass or cup, snipping them with sharp scissors rather than using a knife on a board, where much of the flavour is lost.

1½lb–2lb (750g–1kg) asparagus
4oz (125g) corn salad (lamb's
    lettuce)
1oz (25g) pine nuts, toasted

Sauce
3 egg yolks
2 tablespoons tarragon vinegar

4oz (125g) butter, cut into small
    pieces
pepper
2 teaspoons Pernod
2 tablespoons chopped fresh herbs
    (i.e. chervil, parsley, tarragon,
    chives)

1. Trim and discard the tough ends of the asparagus stalks. Cook gently in simmering salted water until tender (about 15–20 minutes). Meanwhile make the sauce.

2. Place the egg yolks and tarragon vinegar in a bowl over barely simmering water. Heat gently, whisking lightly, until the egg yolks are slightly thickened. Add the butter one piece at a time, whisking continuously, until a thick, glossy sauce is formed. Remove from heat and add pepper, Pernod and herbs. Taste and add salt if necessary.
3. Arrange the asparagus on four warmed plates, and pour a little sauce over each. Garnish with corn salad and sprinkle with pine nuts. Serve without delay.

Serves 4

Fennel Soup

Preparation time: 20 minutes   Cooking time: 40–45 minutes

1 large or 2 small fennel bulbs
1 medium potato, peeled
1oz (25g) butter
3 shallots, chopped finely

1 pint (600ml) vegetable stock
1 tablespoon Pernod
¼ pint (150ml) thick Greek yogurt
salt and pepper

1. Remove the feathery green leaves from the fennel bulb and reserve for garnish. Chop the bulb and potato into small pieces.
2. Heat the butter in a large pan, add the shallots and fry until softened (about 5 minutes). Add the fennel and potato and stir to coat them in the butter. Cover and cook gently for 5 minutes.
3. Add the stock and bring to the boil. Cover and simmer for 25–30 minutes, until the fennel is soft. Put the soup in a blender or food processor and blend until smooth.
4. Return the soup to the pan and stir in the Pernod, yogurt and pepper. Reheat gently, stirring all the time, taste and add salt if necessary. Serve hot, sprinkled with the reserved fennel leaves.

Serves 4

The flavourings for Pernod are still entirely natural, being extracted from fennel and Chinese star-anise. The Pernod research laboratories have produced stronger strains of these plants and now cultivate some of their own crops.

Chicken Liver and Grape Crostini

Preparation time: 25 minutes   Cooking time: 15 minutes

This dish also makes a warm and comforting quick snack.

8oz (250g) chicken livers
4 tablespoons olive oil
4 slices French bread, cut
   diagonally
1 shallot, chopped finely
2oz (50g) seedless grapes, peeled

2 teaspoons Pernod
2 tablespoons stock
dash Worcestershire sauce
salt and pepper
1 tablespoon chopped parsley

1. Rinse and dry the chicken livers, removing any dark patches. Chop into small pieces. Heat half the oil in a frying pan, add the bread and fry on both sides until crisp and golden brown. Drain and keep warm.
2. Add the remaining oil to the pan, add the shallot and fry gently until softened. Add the chicken livers and cook, stirring, until evenly coloured.
3. Stir in the grapes, Pernod, stock, Worcestershire sauce, salt and pepper. Cook gently for 2–3 minutes, until the livers are cooked, but slightly pink inside. Place a slice of fried bread on each serving plate and spoon the livers on top. Sprinkle with parsley.

Serves 4

Avocado and Three Pepper Salad

Preparation time: 20 minutes

To check an avocado is ripe, cradle it in your cupped hand. It should yield to gentle pressure.

The differently-coloured peppers make a beautiful salad to accompany avocado. The peppers can be prepared and dressed well in advance of serving.

1 green pepper
1 red pepper
1 yellow or orange pepper
2 large ripe avocados
paprika, to sprinkle
salad burnet or parsley, to garnish

Dressing
1 tablespoon lemon juice
½ teaspoon Dijon mustard
1 teaspoon Pernod
½ teaspoon clear honey
1 clove garlic, crushed
3 tablespoons olive oil
salt and pepper

To ripen an avocado quickly, put it in a paper bag or a drawer with a ripe banana for a day. (This trick also ripens pears or peaches.)

1. Place the peppers under a hot grill, turning occasionally until the skin is evenly charred. Place in a plastic bag and seal until cool enough to handle, then peel off the skins.
2. Cut the stalks off the peppers and remove the seeds. Cut the flesh into thin strips and mix together in a bowl.
3. Place all the dressing ingredients in a screw-topped jar and shake well until slightly thickened. Pour over the peppers and mix well.
4. Just before serving, halve, stone and peel the avocados. Place an avocado half on each plate and cut lengthwise into thin slices. Press the avocado lightly to fan it out and sprinkle with paprika. Pile some pepper salad on one end. Garnish with salad burnet or parsley and serve immediately.

Serves 4

Above: Avocado and three pepper salad (p.10)   *Below*: Asparagus with woodman's sauce (p.8)

French Vegetable and Cheese Soup

Preparation time: 25 minutes   Cooking time: 45 minutes

This soup really is a meal in itself. The winter vegetables with grated cheese and croutons provide a warming winter treat.

4oz (125g) butter
2 tablespoons olive oil
3 slices white bread, cubed
2 turnips
2 leeks
1 celeriac root
2 carrots

4 potatoes
salt and pepper
1 tablespoon Pernod
1¾ pints (1 litre) chicken stock
½ pint (300ml) milk
4oz (125g) Gruyère cheese, grated

Major Henri Dubied manufactured absinthe, the forerunner of Pernod. He was convinced that absinthe taken in moderation after dinner acted as an aphrodisiac. (Ernest Hemingway later agreed.) Thus began one of many legends surrounding absinthe, but it has never been scientifically proven and was most likely the result of wishful thinking.

1. Melt half the butter with the oil in a large frying pan. Add the bread cubes and fry on all sides until they are crisp and golden brown. Drain on kitchen paper.
2. Peel and cube the turnips. Slice and wash the leeks. Peel and cube the celeriac. Peel and slice the carrots and potatoes.
3. Heat the remaining butter in a large saucepan, add the turnips, leeks, celeriac and carrots. Fry gently for 10 minutes, stirring frequently. Add the potatoes, salt and pepper, Pernod and stock and bring to the boil. Reduce the heat, cover and simmer for 30 minutes, until the vegetables are tender. Stir in the milk and heat through gently.
4. Put the croutons in the base of a soup tureen and sprinkle with the cheese. Pour the soup over and serve piping hot.

Serves 6–8

Fish and Shellfish

Baked Snapper

Preparation time: 40 minutes   Cooking time: 35–40 minutes

Any firm-fleshed fish which is suitable for baking can be used in this recipe. Try sea bream, large red or grey mullet, redfish or sea bass.

1½lb–2lb (750g–1kg) red snapper, scaled, head removed and cut into two fillets (reserve head and bones)
2 carrots, peeled
1 onion, peeled and quartered
a few black peppercorns
1 bay leaf
1 stick celery

4 spring onions
bouquet garni
2 tablespoons Pernod
¼ pint (150ml) dry white wine
4 tablespoons double cream
2oz (50g) butter, cut into small pieces
salt and pepper

1. Place the head and bones of the fish in a saucepan with 1 carrot, the onion, peppercorns, bay leaf and salt. Add water to cover. Bring to the boil slowly, skim off any froth and simmer for 20 minutes. Strain through a fine sieve.
2. Cut the remaining carrot, celery and spring onions into matchstick-sized strips. Sprinkle half over the base of a buttered shallow oven-proof dish. Lay the fish fillets on top and sprinkle with the remaining vegetables. Add the bouquet garni, Pernod and wine. Season with salt and pepper and cover with foil. Bake at 200°C (400°F/Gas Mark 6) for 25–30 minutes, until the fish is tender.
3. Carefully remove the fish and vegetables to a warmed serving dish and keep warm. Strain the cooking liquid into a small saucepan, bring to the boil and reduce by half. Whisk in the cream. Add the butter, one piece at a time, whisking constantly, until the sauce is thick and glossy. Taste and adjust seasoning. Pour over the fish and serve.

Serves 4

When buying whole fish, check that the eyes are bright, the gills are red, the skin is moist and the smell is fresh.

Above: Baked snapper (p.13)   *Below*: Lobster with Madonna sauce (p.15)

Lobster with Madonna Sauce

Preparation time: 25 minutes   Cooking time: 35 minutes

This warm olive oil sauce is unusual for lobster but works very well. It can also be served with other fish, or cold with chicken and salads.

2 cooked lobsters about 1½lb (750g) each
3 tomatoes
1 tablespoon chopped tarragon
1 teaspoon chopped dill
2 teaspoons Pernod

2 cloves garlic, crushed
8 coriander seeds, crushed lightly
7 fl.oz (200ml) olive oil
salt and pepper
2 tablespoons chopped parsley
salad leaves, to garnish

1. Have the fishmonger split the lobsters in half and clean them. Remove all the meat from the lobster shells (keep the shells). Twist off, then crack the claws and remove the meat, using a skewer if necessary. Roughly chop the lobster meat and place in a bowl.
2. Skin, seed and chop the tomatoes. Place them in a saucepan with all the remaining ingredients except the parsley and salad leaves. Bring to the boil, reduce the heat and simmer very gently for 30 minutes, then stir in the parsley.
3. Place the lobster half-shells on four dinner plates. Arrange salad leaves around each. Carefully stir the lobster meat into the sauce and heat gently until warmed through. Pile the lobster and sauce into the shells and serve.

Serves 4

Test the freshness of a lobster by lifting its tail: it should be stiff.

Plaice in Tomato Cups

Preparation time: 20 minutes   Cooking time: 18–20 minutes

This attractive method of serving fish nestling inside tomatoes works well with sole or whiting too. Serve with steamed potatoes.

4 beefsteak tomatoes
8 small plaice fillets
salt and pepper
3oz (75g) butter

1 clove garlic, crushed
3 tablespoons chopped parsley
1 tablespoon Pernod
lemon wedges, to serve

1. Cut each tomato in half and scoop out the seeds and central pulp. Sprinkle with salt and leave upside down to drain. Season the fish and roll them up.
2. Fit one rolled-up fillet inside each tomato half and place in a buttered baking dish. Use 1oz (25g) of the butter to dot the top of each. Cover with buttered greaseproof paper and bake at 200°C (400°F/Gas Mark 6) for 15 minutes.
3. Melt the remaining butter in a small pan, add the garlic and fry for 1 minute. Stir in the parsley and Pernod.

The (genuine) medicinal properties of the herbs contained in absinthe read like a Victorian advert for a cure-all medicine: they stimulated the appetite and kidneys, relieved painful intestinal cramps and flatulence, reduced fevers and suppressed coughs, as well as being a disinfectant.

4. Place two tomato halves on each warmed dinner plate and spoon a little sauce over each. Garnish with lemon wedges.

Serves 4

Monkfish Kebabs

**Preparation time: 30 minutes, plus chilling time
Cooking time: 8–10 minutes**

Monkfish is ideal for kebabs as the firm flesh does not flake when cooked.

Use inexpensive huss (rock salmon) in place of monkfish in recipes such as kebabs and stews where a firm-fleshed fish is required.

*1½lb (750g) monkfish, skinned
1 red pepper
1 green pepper
6–8 thin slices streaky bacon*

*Marinade
1 tablespoon Pernod*

*2 tablespoons lemon juice
2 tablespoons sunflower oil
1 clove garlic, crushed
½ teaspoon paprika
½ teaspoon clear honey
2 teaspoons chopped dill
salt and pepper*

1. Carefully cut the flesh of the fish away from the central bone. Cut the fish into 1 inch (2.5cm) cubes. In a bowl mix together all the marinade ingredients. Add the monkfish and stir until all the pieces are well coated. Chill for 1 hour.

2. Halve the peppers and remove the seeds. Cut them into 1 inch (2.5cm) squares. Run the back of a knife along the bacon slices to stretch them. Cut each piece in half lengthwise. Wrap a piece of bacon around each cube of monkfish.

To make fresh tomato sauce, fry a small, finely chopped onion in a little olive oil until soft. Add a crushed clove of garlic, a tin of chopped tomatoes (or 8 oz fresh tomatoes, peeled and chopped), a teaspoon of sugar and a tablespoon of cider or wine vinegar. Cover and simmer for 15 minutes, adding water if necessary. Season to taste.

3. Thread the ingredients alternately onto four large or eight small skewers. Place on a grill rack and brush with any remaining marinade. Grill for 8–10 minutes, turning and brushing with marinade occasionally, until the bacon is crisp and the fish feels firm. Serve with saffron rice and fresh tomato sauce.

Serves 4

Trout Stuffed with Sorrel

Preparation time: 20 minutes   Cooking time: 15–18 minutes

If sorrel is not available, use young spinach leaves. Buy pink-fleshed trout, as they make a wonderful contrast to the deep green sorrel.

*4 medium-sized trout, filleted
salt and pepper
3oz (75g) butter
12oz (375g) sorrel leaves*

*2 shallots, chopped finely
2 tablespoons Pernod
2 tablespoons dry white wine
2 tablespoons double cream*

Above: Monkfish kebabs (p.16)   *Below*: Halibut with shallot butter sauce (p.18)

New potatoes have even more flavour if you put them into cooking water that is already boiling.

1. Rinse and dry the fish, sprinkling them all over with salt and pepper. Melt half the butter in a saucepan, add the sorrel and cook gently until softened (about 5 minutes). Season with salt and pepper.
2. Sprinkle the shallots over the base of a buttered shallow ovenproof dish. Stuff each pair of fish fillets with sorrel and arrange in the dish. Dot the top of each fish with the remaining butter and pour over the Pernod and wine.
3. Cover the dish with buttered greaseproof paper and bake at 200°C (400°F/Gas Mark 6) for 15–18 minutes, until the trout is cooked. Remove the trout carefully to a warm serving dish. Stir the cream into the pan juices and pour over the fish. Serve hot with new potatoes.

Serves 4

Halibut with Shallot Butter Sauce

Preparation time: 10 minutes   Cooking time: 12–15 minutes

This dish also works well with less expensive cod steaks.

1 pint (600ml) fish stock
4 halibut steaks, about 6oz (175g) each
4 shallots, chopped finely
4 fl.oz (125ml) white wine

1 tablespoon white wine vinegar
4oz (125g) unsalted butter, cut into small pieces
1 tablespoon Pernod
salt and pepper

Top up wine vinegar with small amounts of left-over wine.

1. Place the stock in a wide shallow pan and bring to a simmer. Slide in the fish, cover and poach for 6–8 minutes until the fish is tender. Remove from the heat and keep the fish warm in the liquid while preparing the sauce.
2. Place the shallots in a small pan with the wine and vinegar. Boil until only a tablespoon of liquid remains. Remove the pan from the heat. Add the butter one piece at a time, whisking constantly to make a glossy sauce. If the sauce becomes too thick, return to the heat briefly.
3. Add the Pernod, salt and pepper, and a tablespoon of fish cooking liquid. Lift the fish from the stock and transfer to warmed dinner plates. Spoon the sauce over the top and serve.

Serves 4

Scampi Montmartre

Preparation time: 20 minutes   Cooking time: 45 minutes

Scampi are really the tail meat of large Dublin Bay prawns. They are usually available frozen and should be thawed slowly before use.

¼ pint (150ml) fish stock
1 tablespoon Pernod
24 peeled scampi (thawed if frozen)
2oz (50g) butter
1 small onion, chopped finely
2 cloves garlic, crushed

1lb (500g) tomatoes, skinned,
*   seeded and chopped*
½ teaspoon sugar
salt and pepper
1 tablespoon tomato purée
1 tablespoon chopped parsley

1. Heat together the stock and Pernod in a frying pan. Add the scampi, cover and poach gently for 3–5 minutes, according to size. Remove scampi with a slotted spoon. Strain the liquid and reserve.

2. Melt the butter in a saucepan, add the onion and garlic and fry until softened but not browned (about 5 minutes). Add the reserved stock, tomatoes, sugar, pepper and tomato purée. Bring to the boil, then simmer uncovered for 30 minutes until thickened, stirring occasionally. Add salt if necessary.

To skin tomatoes, place them in a bowl and cover with boiling water. Leave for 2 minutes, then drain and peel off skins.

3. Add the scampi and parsley to the sauce and heat through gently. Serve with rice or noodles.

Serves 4

Sea Bass and Salmon en Papillote

Preparation time: 35 minutes   Cooking time: 10 minutes

Cooking fish in a paper case traps all its wonderful flavours and aromas.

one 2lb (1kg) sea bass, filleted and
*   skinned*
one 2lb (1kg) salmon tail or small
*   salmon, filleted and skinned*
1 fennel bulb
small bunch parsley
small bunch tarragon
handful of dill sprigs

½ teaspoon grated lemon rind
4 tablespoons Pernod
4 tablespoons lemon juice
2oz (50g) butter
salt
2 teaspoons pink peppercorns,
*   crushed lightly*

1. Cut each fish into 6 equal sized pieces, i.e. each fillet into three. Cut the fennel into quarters, remove the root, then finely slice the bulb. Cook the fennel in boiling salted water for 10 minutes until tender. Drain.

2. Finely chop together the parsley, tarragon and dill. Place in a bowl with the fennel and lemon rind and mix well. Cut six 12 inch (30cm) circles of greaseproof paper and butter them on one side.

To skin a fish fillet, slip a sharp knife between the flesh and skin at the tail end. Grasp the skin firmly with kitchen paper and hold the knife at an angle of 45 degrees. Cut between the flesh and skin using a sawing action.

3. Spoon the fennel mixture over half of the buttered side of each piece of paper. Place a piece of salmon and bass on top and sprinkle with the Pernod and lemon juice, mixed together. Dot the top of each piece of fish with butter, sprinkle with salt and pink peppercorns.

4. Fold each piece of paper in half and double fold and crimp the edges

Above: Scampi Montmartre (p.18)   *Below*: Sea bass and salmon en papillote (p.19)

together to seal. Place on two baking sheets and bake at 200°C (400°F/Gas Mark 6) for 10 minutes. Place each parcel on a warmed dinner plate and allow your guests to open them.

Serves 6

Red Mullet with Vine Leaves

**Preparation time: 20 minutes, plus chilling time
Cooking time: 18–20 minutes**

If fresh vine leaves are not available use the ones sold in brine. Rinse thoroughly and soak in hot water for 30 minutes to remove the excess salt.

4 cleaned red mullet, about 8–10oz
  (250g–300g) each
12–15 vine leaves
3 tablespoons olive oil
1 tablespoon Pernod

1 tablespoon lemon juice
salt and pepper
4oz (125g) butter
1 teaspoon chopped parsley
1 teaspoon Pernod

1. Wrap each mullet in vine leaves and place in a shallow dish. Mix together the olive oil, Pernod, lemon juice, salt and pepper and pour over the fish. Chill for about 1 hour or longer if possible.
2. Soften the butter and beat in the parsley and Pernod. Shape into a roll, wrap in foil and chill until needed.
3. Place the fish in an ovenproof dish and pour over the marinade. Bake uncovered at 200°C (400°F/Gas Mark 6) for 18–20 minutes, until the fish is tender. Transfer to warmed plates and serve with slices of Pernod butter.

Serves 4

Wrap whole fish in vine leaves before barbecuing. The leaves impart a wonderful flavour, the fish stays moist and when the leaves are peeled back, the skin comes away too.

Red Mullet with Star Anise and Orange

Preparation time: 45 minutes   Cooking time: 20–25 minutes

When buying your mullet, ask the fishmonger to leave in the liver, as it is a delicacy.

3 star anise
$\frac{1}{2}$ pint (300ml) water
2 tablespoons olive oil
1 tablespoon Pernod
1 carrot, peeled
1 leek

2 oranges
2 tomatoes
4 cleaned red mullet, about 8–10oz
  (250g–300g) each
1 teaspoon green peppercorns
salt

Star anise comes from a tree grown in China, and is related to the magnolia. It is particularly good with duck or pork and is an essential ingredient of Chinese five-spice powder.

1. Place the star anise and water in a small saucepan and bring slowly to the boil. Remove from the heat, cover and leave to infuse for 30 minutes. Strain and stir in the olive oil and Pernod.
2. Cut the carrot and leek into fine matchstick-sized pieces. Remove the peel and white pith from the oranges, then cut the flesh into thick slices. Skin the tomatoes and cut them into eight wedges.
3. Sprinkle half the vegetables and orange over the base of a frying pan large enough to take the mullet. Arrange the fish on top and scatter the rest of the vegetables over them. Sprinkle with peppercorns and salt, and pour the infusion over.
4. Bring slowly to the boil, then cover tightly with a lid or foil and simmer for 15–20 minutes, until the mullet are cooked and the vegetables are tender.

Serves 4

Sole with Bananas

Preparation time: 15 minutes, plus chilling time
Cooking time: 15–18 minutes

Try this dish with other white fish such as plaice or whiting.

4 large lemon sole fillets
2 tablespoons seasoned flour
1 large egg
½ teaspoon chopped tarragon
salt and pepper
4oz (125g) fresh white breadcrumbs

3oz (75g) butter
2 tablespoons oil
2 ripe bananas
3 tablespoons lemon juice
2 tablespoons Pernod
lemon slices and parsley, to garnish

1. Coat the fish in seasoned flour. Beat together the egg, tarragon, salt and pepper. Coat the fish in the egg, then in breadcrumbs to completely cover the pieces. Chill for 30 minutes.
2. Heat the butter and oil in a large frying pan. Add the fish and fry for 6–8 minutes, turning once (fry them in batches if necessary). Transfer to a warmed serving plate and keep warm.
3. Peel the bananas, cut in half lengthwise, then in half across. Add to the pan with the lemon juice and Pernod. Heat the bananas gently in the sauce for 5 minutes, turning occasionally. Arrange the bananas on the dish and spoon a little sauce over them. Garnish with parsley and lemon slices.

Serves 4

Rock Salmon Pernodette

Preparation time: 25 minutes   Cooking time: 30–35 minutes

Rock salmon is also called huss in some parts of the country. Serve this dish with rice or steamed potatoes.

Above: Red mullet with vine leaves (p.21)   *Below*: Red mullet with star anise and orange (p.21)

Above: Cod with piquant sauce (p.25)   *Below*: Rock salmon Pernodette (p.22)

¾ pint (450ml) fish stock
12 pickling onions, peeled
1 bunch baby carrots, peeled
4oz (125g) button mushrooms
4 pieces rock salmon, about 6oz
  (175g) each
pinch powdered saffron

2 tablespoons Pernod
1oz (25g) butter
1oz (25g) plain flour
3 tablespoons double cream
salt and pepper
sprigs of dill, to garnish

1. Heat the stock in a frying pan, add the onions and cook gently for 10 minutes. Add the carrots and mushrooms and cook for a further 5 minutes. Remove vegetables with a slotted spoon and keep warm.
2. Add the fish to the stock, cover and cook gently until tender (about 10 minutes). Remove carefully using a fish slice and keep warm. Strain the stock into a jug and add the saffron and Pernod.
3. Melt the butter in a saucepan, add the flour and cook for 1 minute. Gradually stir in the stock, cooking until the sauce is thick, smooth and glossy. Stir in the cream, salt and pepper and heat through.
4. Arrange the fish and vegetables on four warmed plates. Pour the sauce over and garnish with dill.

Serves 4

Cod with Piquant Sauce

Preparation time: 30 minutes   Cooking time: 25 minutes

1½lb (750g) cod fillet, skinned
1 tablespoon seasoned flour
5 tablespoons oil
1 medium onion, chopped finely
2 teaspoons plain flour
4 tomatoes, peeled, seeded and
  chopped

½ green pepper, chopped
¼ pint (150ml) dry white wine
¼ pint (150ml) water
1 tablespoon Pernod
salt and pepper
12 stuffed olives
chopped parsley, to garnish

1. Rinse and dry the fish, cut into 4 equal-sized pieces and dust with seasoned flour.
2. Heat 1 tablespoon of the oil in a saucepan, add the onion and fry until softened (about 5 minutes). Stir in the plain flour and cook for 1 minute. Add the tomatoes, green pepper, wine, water and Pernod and bring to the boil, stirring all the time. Cover and cook gently for 10 minutes, stirring occasionally.
3. Meanwhile, heat the remaining oil in a large frying pan. Add the fish and fry for 4–5 minutes on each side, turning the fish carefully once.
4. Taste and season the sauce, then add the olives and heat through. Pour a little sauce onto each dinner plate and place a piece of fish on top. Sprinkle with parsley and serve with small new potatoes.

Serves 4

Use your microwave to skin peppers quickly and easily. Cut the pepper into quarters, cook on full power for 1–2 minutes, then peel off skin.

Rolled Sole Fillets in Pernod and Prawn Sauce

Preparation time: 25 minutes   Cooking time: 18–20 minutes

Delicately flavoured sole needs careful cooking to preserve its taste and moist texture, so time it carefully.

1oz (25g) butter
4oz (125g) button mushrooms,
  chopped finely
2 shallots, chopped finely
1 tablespoon snipped chives
2oz (50g) fresh white breadcrumbs
1 tablespoon Pernod
2 tablespoons lemon juice

salt and pepper
6 large lemon sole fillets
¼ pint (150ml) fish or vegetable
  stock
4 tablespoons double cream
4oz (125g) peeled prawns
chives, to garnish

1. Melt the butter in a small pan. Add the mushrooms and shallots and cook for 2–3 minutes, until softened. Mix well with the chives, breadcrumbs, Pernod, lemon juice, salt and pepper.
2. Cut each sole fillet in half lengthwise. Spread each piece with a little stuffing, roll up and secure with a cocktail stick. Place the rolls in one layer in a buttered shallow ovenproof dish. Pile any remaining stuffing onto the centre of each roll. Pour the stock over and cover with a piece of buttered greaseproof paper. Bake at 190°C (375°F/Gas Mark 5) for 12–15 minutes, until tender.
3. Transfer the fish to a warmed serving plate and keep warm. Strain the cooking juices into a small pan and bring to the boil. Add the cream and prawns and heat through gently. Taste and add salt and pepper if necessary. Serve the rolls with prawn sauce and garnish with chives.

Serves 4

From 1844 to 1847 French troops were busy suppressing a tribal uprising in Algeria. To preserve the men from malaria, they were issued with a daily ration of Pernod, added to their wine.

Above: Sole with bananas (p.22)   *Below*: Rolled sole fillets in Pernod and prawn sauce (p.26)

Above: Steak with mustard sauce (p.29)   *Below*: Ribbons of steak Pernodine (p.29)

Main Meals and Accompaniments

Steak with Mustard Sauce

Preparation time: 10 minutes, plus marinating time
Cooking time: 15–20 minutes

A delicious dish which gives maximum effect with minimum fuss.

4 fillet steaks, about 6oz (175g)
  each
2 teaspoons olive oil
salt and pepper
1oz (25g) butter

2 shallots, chopped finely
2 teaspoons Dijon mustard
1 tablespoon Pernod
¼ pint (150ml) double cream
¼ pint (150ml) single cream

1. Rub the steaks with oil, salt and pepper. Leave for 30 minutes to marinate. Melt the butter in a frying pan, add the shallots and fry gently until softened (about 5 minutes). Increase the heat and add the steaks, cooking them for 3–4 minutes on each side depending on taste. Remove from the pan and keep warm.
2. Add the mustard and Pernod to the pan juices and mix well. Add the cream a little at a time and cook gently until thickened and just bubbling. Taste and add salt and pepper if needed.
3. Return the steaks to the pan and heat through in the sauce, turning them once. Serve hot.

Serves 4

Pernod was the subject of a well-known painting by the legendary Pablo Picasso in 1912. Simply entitled *Bottle of Pernod (table in a café)*, the painting is an example of the Analytical Cubism style, in which the same object is seen from different angles, with the images combined and superimposed, often in a complex form. The painting (oil on canvas) can be seen in the Hermitage Museum in Leningrad where it has been since 1948.

Ribbons of Steak Pernodine

Preparation time: 25 minutes, plus marinating time
Cooking time: 20 minutes

Full-flavoured fresh tomatoes are best for this dish. In the winter, when fresh tomatoes lack taste, use a 14oz (400g) can instead.

1lb (500g) rump steak
salt and pepper
3 tablespoons Pernod
1 tablespoon olive oil
1oz (25g) butter

2 onions, chopped finely
1lb (500g) tomatoes, skinned,
    seeded and chopped
1 teaspoon chopped marjoram

1. Cut the steak into strips $\frac{1}{2}$ inch (1cm) wide, using a large sharp knife. Place in a bowl with salt, pepper and Pernod. Mix well and leave for 1 hour.
2. Heat the oil and butter in a large frying pan. Add the onions and fry until softened (about 5 minutes). Add the steak and fry quickly until browned. Stir in the tomatoes and marjoram and cook gently for 10 minutes, stirring occasionally. Taste and add salt and pepper if necessary. Serve with noodles.

Serves 4

Pork and Veal Picnic Pie

Preparation time: 35 minutes, plus resting time
Cooking time: 45 minutes

Serve with new potato salad and crunchy raw vegetables.

Pastry
8oz (250g) plain flour
a pinch of salt
4oz (125g) butter, softened
3 fl.oz (75ml) water

Filling
1 egg white, lightly whisked

8oz (250g) pork fillet
8oz (250g) pie veal
1 medium onion, chopped finely
2 tablespoons chopped parsley
1 clove garlic, chopped finely
2 tablespoons Pernod
salt, black pepper
pinch of nutmeg

1. Sift flour and salt into a bowl. Make a well in the centre and into this put the butter and water. Mix with fingertips, gradually blending the flour with butter and water. Knead for 4–5 minutes. Roll into a ball, cover with a damp cloth and leave in the refrigerator or very cool place for 2 hours before using.
2. Line a 7 inch (18cm) pie tin with just over half the pastry. Seal the pastry with egg white to prevent the filling making it soggy. Mince the meats and add the onion, parsley, garlic, Pernod and seasoning. Knead together for a few minutes, mixing well.
3. Shape mixture into balls about the size of golf balls, and arrange in the pastry case, leaving a little space between them. Roll out the remaining pastry for the top. Dampen the edges of the lining with cold water. Pinch edges together and seal well. Make two or three cuts in the top to allow the steam to escape. Brush the top with egg white. Bake for 45 minutes at 180°C (350°F/Gas Mark 4) until deep golden brown. Serve warm or cold.

Serves 4

Every picture tells a story, and the Pernod label is no exception. The 'leaf' background reflects the importance of herbs in its recipe, and the tiny Swiss cap perched atop the brand logo commemorates the fact that Pernod was first made in Switzerland.

Above: Poussin Pernodine (p.32)   *Below*: Pork kebabs with Pernod tomato sauce (p.32)

Poussin Pernodine

Preparation time: 25 minutes Cooking time: 45–50 minutes

Poussin makes a delicious alternative to chicken, at little extra cost.

1 teaspoon fennel seeds
1 teaspoon mixed dried herbs
1 tablespoon chopped parsley
salt and freshly ground black pepper
2 tablespoons oil
4 poussin
½ pint (300ml) chicken stock

1 tablespoon Pernod
2 egg yolks
¼ pint (150ml) single cream
1oz (25g) butter, cut into small
   pieces
2 tablespoons chopped parsley
1 teaspoon grated lemon rind

By the 1890s, Pernod was *de rigeur* amongst the Bohemian circles on the Parisian Left Bank. The artists would sit in the cafés for hours sipping Pernod, and it even became the subject of paintings by Degas, Picasso, and Toulouse-Lautrec.

1. Mix together the fennel seeds, mixed herbs, parsley, salt and pepper. Sprinkle the mixture over the inside and outside of the poussin.
2. Heat the oil in a large casserole, add the poussin and fry on all sides until golden brown. Add the stock and Pernod and bring to the boil. Reduce the heat, cover and cook gently for 40–45 minutes until the poussin are tender.
3. Remove the poussin from the stock and keep warm while preparing the sauce. Blend together the egg yolks and cream, add to the stock and cook gently, stirring, until the sauce is thickened. Do not allow to boil. Add the butter, one piece at a time, stirring constantly. Taste and adjust seasoning if necessary.
4. Mix the parsley and lemon rind. Place each poussin on a plate, pour the sauce around it and sprinkle with parsley and lemon.

Serves 4

Pork Kebabs with Pernod Tomato Sauce

Preparation time: 30 minutes Cooking time: 15–18 minutes

1½lb (750g) lean pork
4oz (125g) button mushrooms
6oz (175g) cherry tomatoes
4–8 bay leaves
2 tablespoons lemon juice
1 tablespoon Pernod
4 tablespoons olive oil
salt and pepper

½ teaspoon oregano
Sauce
1 small onion, chopped finely
1 stick celery, chopped finely
14oz (400g) can chopped tomatoes
1 tablespoon Pernod
1 teaspoon sugar
1 tablespoon tomato purée

1. Cut the pork into 1 inch (2.5cm) cubes. Thread the meat alternately with the mushrooms, tomatoes and bay leaves onto 4 large skewers.
2. Whisk together the lemon juice, Pernod, olive oil, salt, pepper and oregano. Brush over the kebabs and grill them for 15–18 minutes,

turning occasionally. Brush with the marinade each time you turn the kebabs. Meanwhile make the sauce.

3. Place all the sauce ingredients in a saucepan, bring to the boil and simmer uncovered for 10–12 minutes, until thickened. Taste and add salt and pepper. Serve the kebabs and sauce with rice.

Serves 4

Pork Pernodette

Preparation time: 15 minutes Cooking time: 20 minutes

4 boneless pork steaks
salt and pepper
2oz (50g) fine dried white
  breadcrumbs
1 teaspoon dried sage
1 beaten egg
1oz (25g) butter
1 tablespoon sunflower oil

1 teaspoon flour
½ pint (300ml) passata (sieved
  tomatoes)
¼ pint (150ml) vegetable stock
pinch sugar
1 tablespoon Pernod
salt and freshly ground black pepper

1. Place the steaks between two sheets of non-stick baking parchment and beat flat with a rolling pin. Season on both sides with salt and pepper. Mix together the breadcrumbs and sage. Dip the steaks in beaten egg, then toss in the breadcrumbs and sage mixture to coat.
2. Heat the butter and oil together in a frying pan. Fry the pork gently on both sides until tender and browned. Drain well and keep warm.
3. Add the flour to the pan and cook for 1 minute. Stir in the passata, stock, sugar, Pernod, salt and pepper. Bring to the boil, then simmer for 5 minutes. Pour into a jug and serve with the pork. Sauté potatoes and creamed spinach are particularly good accompaniments.

Serves 4

Veal Steaks à la Marseillaise

Preparation time: 25 minutes Cooking time: 30 minutes

Veal cutlets can be used instead of steaks in this recipe. If salsify is not available, use celery instead.

2oz (50g) shelled pistachio nuts
1lb (500g) salsify
4oz (125g) butter
4 veal steaks from the loin or leg,
  about 5oz (150g) each
salt and pepper

2 teaspoons flour
1 tablespoon chopped parsley
3 tablespoons Pernod
¼ pint (150ml) chicken or veal stock
3 fl.oz (75ml) double cream
pinch powdered saffron

Salsify is also known as the oyster plant because of the flavour of its long tapering roots. It is in season in the autumn and winter.

Above: Veal steaks à la Marseillaise (p.33)   *Below*: Blanquette of veal Pernodine (p.35)

1. Cover the pistachios with boiling water, leave for 5 minutes, then drain and slip off the skins. Chop roughly. Peel the salsify and chop into 2 inch (5cm) lengths, boil until tender (about 15 minutes), then drain.
2. Heat half the butter in a frying pan. Coat the veal in salt, pepper and flour and add to the pan. Fry for 8 minutes each side. Transfer to a warmed dish and keep warm.
3. Add the remaining butter to the pan, add the salsify and fry gently for 2–3 minutes. Sprinkle with parsley and keep warm in a dish.
4. Add the Pernod and stock to the pan and boil until reduced by half. Reduce the heat, add the cream and saffron and simmer for 5 minutes. Taste and adjust seasoning. Serve the veal surrounded by the salsify. Pour the sauce over and sprinkle with pistachios.

Serves 4

Blanquette of Veal Pernodine

Preparation time: 30 minutes   Cooking time: 1¾ hours

This dish can be made using pork instead of veal, but you will need to reduce the main cooking time to 45 minutes.

1½lb (750g) stewing veal
2 onions
2 cloves
1 bouquet garni
1 pint (600ml) chicken or vegetable
 stock
2oz (50g) butter
1½oz (40g) plain flour
1 tablespoon Pernod

¼ pint (150ml) milk
4oz (125g) button mushrooms
salt and pepper
¼ pint (150ml) single cream
1 egg yolk
6 rashers streaky bacon, rind
 removed
chopped parsley, to garnish

1. Cut the veal into 1 inch (2.5cm) cubes. Cut one onion in half and stud each half with a clove. Place the veal, onion halves, bouquet garni and stock in a saucepan and bring gently to the boil. Cover and simmer for 1½ hours until the meat is tender. Strain and reserve the stock.
2. Chop the remaining onion. Melt the butter in a large saucepan, add the onion and fry gently until softened (about 5 minutes). Stir in the flour and cook for 1 minute. Gradually add the stock, stirring until thickened and smooth.
3. Add the veal to the pan with the Pernod, milk and mushrooms and simmer for 5 minutes. Taste and add salt and pepper. Blend the cream with the egg yolk and add to the pan. Reheat gently, taking care not to let the liquid boil.
4. Cut each bacon rasher in half, roll up and pin with a cocktail stick. Grill on all sides until evenly browned (about 6 minutes). Garnish the veal dish with bacon rolls and parsley.

Make your own bouquet garni from sprigs of fresh herbs such as rosemary, thyme and parsley, plus a bay leaf. Wrap them in a 3 inch strip of green leaf from a leek (or use the bay leaf) and tie with string at the top and bottom.

Serves 4

Chicken Breasts with Asparagus and Pernod Sauce

Preparation time: 20 minutes   Cooking time: 25–30 minutes

This delicate sauce is perfect with chicken or white fish.

8oz (250g) thin asparagus spears
2 teaspoons seasoned plain flour
4 boneless chicken breasts, about
  4oz (125g) each
1oz (25g) butter
2 shallots, chopped finely

½ pint (300ml) chicken stock
1 small potato, peeled and chopped
  finely
1 tablespoon Pernod
salt and pepper

If your sauce or gravy tastes a little thin, whisk in small knobs of butter to thicken and enrich it while giving it a glossy sheen.

1. Cut off the asparagus tips and set aside. Peel and thinly slice the stalks. Coat the chicken breasts with the seasoned flour.
2. Heat the butter in a large frying pan with a lid. Add the chicken and fry quickly on both sides until golden brown. Remove from the pan. Add the shallots to the pan and fry gently until softened. Add the asparagus stalks and fry for a further 2 minutes. Add the stock, potato, Pernod, salt and pepper and bring to the boil.
3. Return the chicken to the pan, cover and simmer for 10–12 minutes, until the vegetables are cooked and the chicken is tender.
4. Meanwhile, cook the asparagus tips in boiling salted water for 4–5 minutes, until just tender. Drain and keep warm.
5. Using a slotted spoon, transfer the chicken breasts to warmed serving plates. Purée the sauce in a blender or food processor and pour around the chicken. Garnish with asparagus tips and serve with new potatoes and a green salad.

Serves 4

Braised Duck with Pernod

Preparation time: 25 minutes   Cooking time: 25 minutes

Boneless duck breasts are good value as whole ducks contain a lot of bone. This is a succulent method of cooking.

4 boneless duck breasts, 6–8oz
  (175g–250g) each
1 tablespoon sunflower oil
1 onion, chopped
2 carrots, chopped
3 fl.oz (75ml) white wine
2 tablespoons Pernod

½ teaspoon grated orange rind
3 tablespoons fresh orange juice
4 tablespoons soured cream
1 teaspoon cornflour
salt and pepper
mint, to garnish

1. Rinse and thoroughly dry the duck breasts. Heat the oil in a flame-proof casserole, add the duck breasts skin side down, and fry until

Above: Chicken breasts with asparagus and Pernod sauce (p.36)   *Below*: Braised duck with Pernod (p.36)

Above: Beetroot and red onion salad (p.40)   *Below*: Baked cabbage with Pernod (p.39)

well browned. Turn and fry on the other side to seal. Remove and drain on kitchen paper.

2. Add the onion and carrot to the pan and fry until softened (about 5 minutes). Add the wine and Pernod and stir well, scraping any sediment from the base of the pan. Add the orange rind, juice, salt and pepper and bring to the boil.

3. Return the duck to the pan, cover and cook gently for 20 minutes, until the duck is tender. Remove the duck and keep warm.

4. Skim any fat from the surface of the cooking juices using a tablespoon, purée in a blender or food processor and return to the pan. Blend the soured cream and cornflour and stir into the sauce, cooking gently until thickened. Add salt and pepper if necessary.

5. Thinly slice the duck meat and serve on a pool of sauce on warmed plates. Garnish with mint.

Serves 4

To skim excess fat from the surface of soups, gravies or stews lay strips of kitchen paper on the surface, lift and discard. The paper absorbs the fat but the liquid (and flavour) runs off.

Baked Cabbage with Pernod

Preparation time: 35 minutes   Cooking time: 45 minutes

Serve this on its own as a warming supper dish, or as an accompaniment to game or roast beef.

1 tablespoon olive oil
2 onions, peeled and sliced thinly
5oz (150g) smoked streaky bacon,
  chopped
1½lb (750g) white cabbage, shredded
  finely

2 cloves garlic, crushed
salt and pepper
2 eggs
¼ pint (150ml) milk
1 tablespoon Pernod
2 tablespoons dried breadcrumbs

1. Heat the oil in a large pan, add the onions and fry gently until softened and lightly browned (about 10 minutes). Add the bacon and fry for 5 minutes, stirring occasionally.

2. Add the cabbage, garlic, salt and pepper. Stir well to mix. Cover and cook gently for 20 minutes.

3. Beat together the eggs, milk and Pernod. Transfer the cabbage mixture to a buttered gratin dish. Pour over the egg and milk mixture. Sprinkle with breadcrumbs and bake at 160°C (325°F/Gas Mark 3) for 45 minutes. Serve hot.

Serves 4–6

In scientific terms, Pernod turns milky when water is added because the essential oils and resins from the herbal extracts are precipitated out of the alcohol and remain in suspension to form an emulsion.

Pernod Pork Chops

Preparation time: 15 minutes, plus marinating time
Cooking time: 20–25 minutes

4 pork chops
salt and freshly ground black pepper
2 tablespoons Pernod
1 tablespoon olive oil

2 cloves garlic, chopped
¼ pint (150ml) hot vegetable or
  chicken stock

In Ancient Egypt, anise was believed to cure cardiac disease. In fact, its medicinal properties include the relief of intestinal disorders, the suppression of coughs and the stimulation of the milk glands.

1. Season chops with salt and pepper and put in a dish. Dribble half the Pernod over the chops, cover and refrigerate for several hours, or overnight if possible.
2. Heat the oil in a frying pan with a lid, add the chops and brown quickly on both sides. Stir in the garlic, hot stock and remaining Pernod.
3. Cover the pan and cook the chops gently for 20–25 minutes, adding a little more stock if necessary. Serve with sauté potatoes and creamed spinach or broccoli.

Serves 4

Beetroot and Red Onion Salad

Preparation time: 20 minutes

Choose young, tender beetroot for this salad.

12oz (350g) small uncooked
   beetroots
2 celery sticks
1 red onion
1 orange

Dressing
¼ pint (150ml) thick Greek yogurt
1 teaspoon clear honey
1 tablespoon chopped parsley
1 tablespoon chopped spring onions
1 teaspoon Pernod
salt and pepper

1. Peel the beetroots and grate them into a bowl. Finely chop the celery. Peel and thinly slice the onion. Peel the orange, removing all the white pith. Cut into segments and chop. Add these ingredients to the beetroot and mix well.
2. Mix together all the dressing ingredients until well blended. Arrange the salad in bowls and spoon the dressing over the top.

Serves 4

Rabbit with Glazed Turnips

Preparation time: 30 minutes   Cooking time: 45 minutes

Skinned chicken pieces can be used instead of rabbit if preferred.

3lb (1.5kg) rabbit pieces
2 teaspoons flour
salt and pepper
1oz (25g) butter
¼ pint (150ml) chicken stock
8oz (250g) fresh spinach, shredded

1lb (500g) baby turnips
2oz (50g) butter
2 teaspoons sugar
2 teaspoons Pernod
1oz (25g) softened butter, cut into
   small pieces

1. Dust the rabbit with flour, salt and pepper. Heat the butter in a flameproof casserole, add the rabbit and fry on all sides until evenly browned. Cover and cook over a moderate heat for 5 minutes.
2. Add the stock and bring to the boil. Cover and reduce the heat to a simmer. After 20 minutes, add the spinach, stir well and continue

Above: Fillet roast with cucumbers (p.42)   *Below*: Rabbit with glazed turnips (p.40)

cooking for a further 10 minutes, until the rabbit is tender.

3. Whilst the rabbit cooks, peel the turnips, leaving a tuft of green top on each. Place in a frying pan with enough water to just cover. Add the butter, sugar, salt and pepper and bring to the boil. Cook uncovered for 16–18 minutes, until the water has evaporated. Shake the pan occasionally to turn the turnips in the syrupy mixture.

4. Using a slotted spoon, remove the rabbit and spinach from the pan and keep warm. Boil the cooking liquid until only 2 tablespoons remain. Add the Pernod and beat in the butter, one piece at a time. Pour the sauce over the rabbit and serve with the turnips.

Serves 4

Fillet Roast with Cucumbers

Preparation time: 30 minutes   Cooking time: 30 minutes

Leave a roast joint to stand at room temperature for 20 minutes before carving. The juices that are drawn to the surface during cooking will sink back into the centre, making the meat moist all the way through.

This extra-tender lean cut of beef needs larding to prevent it drying out during cooking. Ask the butcher to do this for you.

1¾lb fillet of beef, larded
　for roasting
1oz (25g) butter, softened
2 tablespoons oil
1 medium cucumber
1oz (25g) butter
½ red pepper, diced

3 shallots, chopped finely
7 fl.oz (200ml) beef stock
2 teaspoons Pernod
2 tablespoons double cream
2oz (50g) butter, cut into small
　pieces
salt and pepper

1. Preheat the oven to 230°C (450°F/Gas Mark 8). Dry the beef with kitchen paper. Rub the beef with the softened butter and brush with oil. Place in a tin and roast in the oven for 20 minutes, then remove from the oven. Cover the meat with foil and allow to sit for 10 minutes, so that it will be evenly pink all the way through.

2. Peel the cucumber and cut it into matchstick-sized slivers. Plunge into boiling water, parboil for 1 minute, then drain. Melt half the butter in a frying pan and sauté the cucumber until tender and beginning to brown. Sauté the red pepper in the remaining butter.

3. Transfer the roast from the roasting pan onto a platter, and place in the warm oven while preparing the sauce.

4. On top of the stove, brown the shallots in the roasting pan, then add the stock and Pernod, scraping the sediment from the tin. Stir all the pan juices into the liquid, bring to the boil, and allow to reduce by a third. Add the cream, then remove from the heat and add the butter, a few pieces at a time, whisking the sauce vigorously. Taste for seasoning and add salt and pepper if necessary. Add the cucumber and red pepper to the sauce. Slice the beef thickly and serve with sauce and new potatoes.

Serves 4

42

Desserts

Oriental Fruit Salad

Preparation time: 30 minutes, plus chilling time

Mix and match whichever exotic fruits are in season.

2 star fruit
8oz (250g) lychees
8 kumquats
2 kiwi fruit

1 mango
2 tablespoons fresh lime juice
2 tablespoons caster sugar
1 tablespoon Pernod

1. Trim along the lengths of all the points on the star fruit, slice thinly and remove any pips with the point of a knife. Peel and stone the lychees. Slice the kumquats. Peel and slice the kiwi fruit. Peel, stone and chop the mango.
2. Mix together all the fruits in a bowl. Sprinkle over the lime juice, sugar and Pernod and stir well. Chill for at least 1 hour before serving.

Serves 4

To cut the flesh from a mango, lay it flat and cut through horizontally as close to the stone as possible. Turn the fruit over, and cut in the same way. Remove the remaining flesh from the stone.

Banana Fritters

Preparation time: 30 minutes   Cooking time: 8–10 minutes

4oz (125g) plain flour
1oz (25g) granulated sugar
1 egg
pinch of salt
½ pint (300ml) milk
4 ripe bananas
2 tablespoons Pernod
4oz (125g) sugar

flour, to coat bananas
oil, for deep frying
6 tablespoons water

To serve
4 bowls iced water
ice cubes
1 teaspoon Pernod per bowl

1. To make the batter, place the flour, 1oz of sugar and salt in bowl. Make a well in the centre, drop the egg in and gradually add the milk,

Above: Oriental fruit salad (p.43) *Below*: Banana fritters (p.43)

mixing with a wooden spoon and drawing in the flour until you have a smooth batter. Do not overbeat.

2. To make the fritters, peel the bananas and cut each one into 8 slices. Marinate for 10 minutes in the Pernod and 1 tablespoon of the sugar.
3. Heat the oil in a deep fryer until very hot (300°F/150°C). Remove the bananas from the marinade, roll them in flour to coat lightly, then dip in the batter and deep fry for about 2 minutes. Do this in batches. Lift the fritters out of the fryer and drain on absorbent paper.
4. Place the remaining sugar and the water in a saucepan and heat gently, stirring until the sugar has dissolved. Boil for 2–3 minutes to form a light caramel syrup. Use a fork to dip each fritter into the caramel, coating each one completely. Place the caramelized fritters on an oiled baking sheet (keep them from touching) and keep warm.
5. To serve, place before each guest a bowl containing iced water, several ice cubes and a teaspoon of Pernod. Serve a plate of hot fritters to each guest, who should use a fork to dip the fritters one at a time into the ice water to harden the caramel, and immediately lift them out and eat them.

Serves 4

Pernod's £10 million super-tech complex on the outskirts of Paris is known locally as *La Pernoderie*. Just six men watch over the computer-controlled distilling process, which makes around 300,000 bottles of Pernod (and allied drinks) per day.

Mint and Pernod Parfait

Preparation time: 1 hour, plus cooling and freezing

7oz (200g) granulated sugar
6 tablespoons water
9 egg yolks
¼ pint (150ml) milk

3 tablespoons mint syrup
few drops green food colouring
7 fl.oz (200ml) double cream
3 tablespoons Pernod

1   To make the ice-cream, heat 2oz (50g) of the sugar with the milk in a small pan until the sugar has dissolved. Whisk together 3 of the egg yolks, then whisk in the milk. Cool completely, and beat in the mint syrup and colouring. Pour the mixture into a shallow tray and freeze until just beginning to set. Turn into a chilled bowl, and whisk to break down any large ice crystals. Return to freezer until just firm.
2. Press the ice-cream around the sides and base of a 2 pint (1.2 litre) damp mould or basin. Return to the freezer.
3. Make an egg yolk syrup by placing 4oz (125g) of the sugar in a saucepan with the water. Bring gently to the boil, stirring until the sugar has dissolved. Remove from heat
4. Place the remaining 6 egg yolks in a bowl over a pan of simmering water. Whisk together, then continue whisking as you pour in the hot syrup. Whisk for about 7–8 minutes, until foaming. Remove the bowl from the pan and whisk until cooled.
5. Whisk the cream until stiff, add the remaining sugar, then fold in the egg yolk syrup and Pernod. Pour into the centre of the ice-cream

If you keep your eggs in the fridge, take them out at least 30 minutes before you want to whisk the whites, as warm egg whites whip into a lighter froth and a greater volume than cold.

45

mould and freeze until firm (about 6 hours). Just before serving, dip the mould into hot water and turn out.

Serves 6–8

Pineapple Pernod Ice-cream

Preparation time: 25 minutes, plus freezing time

8oz (250g) can crushed pineapple
2 tablespoons Pernod
4 eggs, separated

4oz (125g) caster sugar
½ pint (300ml) double cream

Whilst Pernod had been known and loved throughout France for more than a century, it was not imported into the UK until 1935.

1. Mix together the pineapple and Pernod. Whisk the egg yolks until light and creamy, then stir in the pineapple mixture.
2. Whisk the egg whites until stiff, then whisk in the sugar, a little at a time. Whip the cream until stiff.
3. Fold the cream into the egg whites, then fold in the fruit. Pour into a rigid shallow container and freeze until firm (about 3 hours).

Serves 4–6

Bavarian Cream with Fruit

Preparation time: 40 minutes, plus chilling time

The fruits used here are chosen for their colours and shapes, but any other seasonal fruit can be substituted.

½ pint (300ml) milk
3oz (75g) granulated sugar
3 egg yolks
1 sachet gelatine
2 tablespoons water
½ pint (300ml) double cream

4 teaspoons Pernod
6oz (175g) strawberries, sliced
3 kiwi fruit, peeled and thinly sliced
2 oranges, peeled and sliced
2 thin slices of pineapple
sprigs of mint

1. Place the milk and half the sugar in a small saucepan and bring to the boil, stirring until the sugar has dissolved. Place the egg yolks and the remaining sugar in a bowl and whisk until the mixture is light and leaves a trail when the whisk is lifted. Pour the milk into the egg mixture and stir well.
2. Return the mixture to the pan, heating gently without boiling, stirring all the time until it thickens to form a custard and lightly coats the back of a spoon. Remove from the heat.

To make the pith of oranges easier to remove, stand the whole fruit in boiling water for 5 minutes before peeling.

3. Sprinkle the gelatine over the water in a small bowl. Place in a pan of simmering water until the gelatine has dissolved. Stir into the hot custard. Allow the mixture to cool completely, stirring occasionally.
4. Whip the cream until stiff. Fold into the custard with the Pernod.

Above: Bavarian cream with fruit (p.46)   *Below*: Red fruits in Pernod syrup (p.48)

Pour into a wetted 1½ pint (900ml) jelly mould and refrigerate until set. Just before serving, dip the mould briefly into very hot water and turn out onto a serving plate. Arrange the sliced strawberries around the edge, and decorate with sprigs of mint. Mix together the remaining fruit and serve separately.

Serves 6–8

Red Fruits in Pernod Syrup

Preparation time: 30 minutes, plus chilling time

Try this delightful fruit salad when soft summer fruits are in abundance.

4oz (125g) granulated sugar
½ pint (300ml) water
1 cinnamon stick
2 tablespoons Pernod

8oz (250g) redcurrants
8oz (250g) blackcurrants
8oz (250g) raspberries
8oz (250g) strawberries, halved

1. Place the sugar, water and cinnamon stick in a saucepan. Bring slowly to the boil, stirring to dissolve the sugar, then boil without stirring for 5 minutes, until the syrup is slightly thickened. Remove the cinnamon stick, add the Pernod, redcurrants and blackcurrants and simmer for 2 minutes. Pour into a bowl and cool.
2. One hour before serving, add the raspberries and strawberries and mix well. Chill until ready to serve.

Serves 4

Pernod and Wine Jelly

Preparation time: 25 minutes, plus chilling time

Choose a light red wine such as Beaujolais or Italian Chianti for this dish.

½ pint (300ml) water
3–4oz (75g–125g) caster sugar
1 sachet powdered gelatine
½ pint (300ml) red wine
3 tablespoons lemon juice

2 tablespoons fresh orange juice
2 tablespoons Pernod
¼ pint (150ml) whipped double
  cream

1. Bring the water to the boil. Add the sugar and stir until dissolved. Simmer for 5 minutes. Remove from the heat and sprinkle in the gelatine. Stir until the gelatine has completely dissolved. Add the wine, lemon and orange juice, and Pernod. Stir well, then strain into a dampened 1½ pint (900ml) jelly mould.
2. Allow to set in the refrigerator overnight. Dip the mould briefly into

Pernod is produced in four French cities (Paris, Lyons, Marseille and Bordeaux), and is exported to 120 countries throughout the world.

48

Above: Ananas crème au Pernod (p.50) *Below*: Apple and Pernod flambé (p.51)

hot water and carefully turn out onto a plate. Decorate the base with rosettes of whipped cream, or serve the cream separately.

Serves 4

Ananas Crême au Pernod

Preparation time: 20 minutes, plus chilling time

Pineapple and Pernod have a natural affinity and this simple dessert has a taste made in heaven.

6oz (175g) cream cheese or curd
   cheese
3oz (75g) caster sugar
2 tablespoons Pernod

1 ripe pineapple
mint, to decorate
ground nutmeg

1. Beat together the cheese, sugar and half the Pernod. Chill for 1 hour.
2. Remove the stalk and top from the pineapple and pare away the skin with a sharp knife. Cut into slices and sprinkle with the remaining Pernod. Serve with the cheese topping and garnish with mint. Sprinkle a light dusting of nutmeg over the top.

Serves 4

Melon Basket
with Pernod Sauce

Preparation time: 30 minutes, plus chilling time

Store melons in the refrigerator in a plastic bag to prevent them from absorbing smells.

1 small watermelon
12oz (375g) black grapes
2 oranges
2 red skinned apples

2 peaches or nectarines
3 tablespoons fresh orange juice
1 tablespoon Pernod
1 tablespoon clear honey

1. Mark a line around the circumference of the melon. Mark a handle over the top, about 1 inch (2.5cm) wide. Using the circumference as a guide, make zigzag cuts with a thin, sharp knife, cutting as deeply as possible. Be sure not to cut through the handle at the sides, and cut straight along the handle lines.
2. Scoop or cut out the flesh from the melon and remove seeds. Cut the flesh into cubes. Halve and seed the grapes. Peel the oranges, removing the white pith. Cut into segments, removing the membrane. Quarter, core and chop the apples. Stone and chop the peaches or nectarines.
3. Mix together all the fruits. Stir together the orange juice, Pernod and

honey, and add to the fruit, stirring gently. Pile into the melon basket and chill until ready to serve.

Serves 4

Pour a little Pernod over a portion of vanilla ice cream and serve immediately for a quick dessert.

Apple and Pernod Flambé

Preparation time: 20 minutes   Cooking time: 10–12 minutes

If you have a fondue pot or spirit burner this dessert can be flambéed at the table. Serve with softly whipped cream or vanilla ice-cream.

2lb (1kg) eating apples (i.e. Cox,
   Worcester Pearmain)
2oz (50g) butter
2oz (50g) soft brown sugar

pinch nutmeg
4 tablespoons fresh orange juice
2 tablespoons Pernod
thin strips of orange peel

1. Peel, core and quarter the apples, then cut each quarter into 3 thick slices. Melt the butter in a frying pan, add the apples and cook gently, turning occasionally until lightly browned but still firm.
2. Add the sugar, nutmeg and orange juice and stir well. Cook gently for 3–5 minutes until the apples are tender. Pour the Pernod quickly over the apples and ignite. Serve when the flames have died down. Decorate with thin strips of orange peel.

Serves 4–6

Pernod is excellent for fruit flambé. Try warming pineapple, banana or orange slices in a pan with butter, sugar and fruit juice. Add Pernod and flambé.

Strawberry and Orange Cups

Preparation time: 20 minutes, plus chilling time

The oranges for this dessert can be prepared the day before and marinated overnight. Stir in the strawberries just before serving.

4 large oranges
2 tablespoons Pernod
1 tablespoon caster sugar

pinch ground cinnamon
8oz (250g) strawberries

1. Cut the oranges in half and using a sharp serrated knife, remove the flesh. (Keep the empty 'shells'.) Discard the membrane and pips and chop the flesh into small pieces. Place the fruit in a bowl with any juice, plus the Pernod, sugar and cinnamon. Stir well and chill for 1 hour, or overnight if you prefer
2. Hull and slice the strawberries. Add to the orange pieces and mix well. To serve, pile the fruit inside the orange shells

Serves 4

Snacks and Drinks

Crudités with Seafood Dip

Preparation time: 30 minutes, plus chilling time

For the dip
4oz (125g) peeled prawns, thawed if
    necessary
2 teaspoons tomato purée
2 teaspoons Pernod
2 teaspoons chopped dill
few shakes Worcestershire sauce
1 tablespoon lemon juice
4 tablespoons mayonnaise
¼ pint (150ml) thick Greek yogurt

salt and pepper

For the crudités
1 small cauliflower
1 red pepper
1 green pepper
3 carrots
1 bunch radishes
3 sticks celery

Dips can be made up to a day in advance and chilled until needed. Prepare the vegetables and store them in polythene bags in the bottom of the fridge for 1 or 2 hours, to make them extra crunchy.

1. Place the prawns in a blender and purée lightly. Add all the remaining dip ingredients and mix well. Turn into a small bowl, cover with clingfilm, and chill until needed.
2. Cut the cauliflower into small florets. Halve the peppers, remove the seeds and cut into strips. Peel the carrots and cut into sticks. Trim the radishes. Cut the celery into sticks.
3. Serve the dip in the centre of a platter, surrounded by the vegetables.

Serves 8–10

Sweetcorn Fritters

Preparation time: 15 minutes   Cooking time: 10–12 minutes

12oz (375g) canned sweetcorn,
    drained
3oz (75g) plain flour
2 tablespoons double cream
4 eggs

1 teaspoon sugar
salt and pepper
2 teaspoons Pernod
oil, for shallow frying

1. Place the corn in a blender or food processor and blend to a smooth purée. Add the flour, cream, eggs, sugar, salt, pepper and Pernod. Blend well.
2. Heat $\frac{1}{2}$ inch (1cm) of oil in a frying pan, add small spoonfuls of batter and fry on both sides until golden. Drain on kitchen paper and keep warm while cooking the remaining fritters.

Serves 6–8

Spear these delicious fritters with cocktail sticks to serve with drinks, or make larger ones as a starter or snack.

Smoked Salmon and Cucumber Rolls

Preparation time: 20 minutes

6oz (175g) sliced smoked salmon
2 teaspoons chopped dill
1 tablespoon Pernod
$\frac{1}{2}$ cucumber
2 teaspoons lemon juice

2 teaspoons snipped chives
salt and pepper
2oz (50g) softened butter
dill, to garnish

1. Separate the salmon slices and sprinkle with dill and Pernod. Peel the cucumber, cut in half lengthwise and scoop out the seeds. Cut each piece into thick cross sections about $1\frac{1}{2}$ inches (4cm) wide. Place in a bowl with the lemon juice, chives, salt and pepper.
2. Spread the salmon with softened butter. Cut into small strips and wrap each strip around a piece of cucumber. Secure with a cocktail stick and transfer to a serving plate. Garnish with dill.

Serves 6–8

You can make these snacks with sliced smoked trout or gravadlax instead of salmon.

Glazed Prawns

Preparation time: 20 minutes   Cooking time: 12–15 minutes

1lb (500g) uncooked large
    Mediterranean prawns, thawed
2 tablespoons oil
2 shallots, chopped finely
salt and pepper

4 tablespoons dry white wine
1 tablespoon Pernod
2 teaspoons chopped dill
1 tablespoon chopped parsley
1 clove garlic, chopped finely

1. Peel the prawns, leaving the tail section intact. Cut down the back and remove the dark intestine. Wash and dry on kitchen paper.
2. Heat the oil in a large pan, add the shallots and fry until softened (about 3 minutes). Add the prawns and fry quickly until pink. Reduce the heat and stir in the salt, pepper, wine, Pernod and dill.
3. Cover and cook gently for 5 minutes, then remove the prawns with a slotted spoon. Keep warm. Reduce the sauce to a coating consistency

These glazed prawns can also be served with a salad as an informal starter.

53

Snacks *(l. to r.)*: Crudités with seafood dip (p.52), Stuffed vegetable canapés (p.56)

Cocktails *(l. to r.)*: Vampire, Pernod Laser, Pernod Iceberg, Monkey Gland (p.57)

and pour over the prawns. Mix together the parsley and garlic and sprinkle over the top. Spear each prawn with a cocktail stick.

Serves 4–6

Stuffed Vegetable Canapés

Preparation time: 30 minutes

1lb (500g) cherry tomatoes
8oz (250g) button mushrooms
6 sticks celery
½ cucumber
8oz (250g) cream cheese or curd
    cheese

2 teaspoons Pernod
1 tablespoon chopped fresh herbs
    (i.e. parsley, tarragon, chives)
salt and pepper

1. Using a small sharp knife, cut the tops off the tomatoes and scoop out the centres using a teaspoon handle. Drain upside down. Remove the stalks from the mushrooms. Cut the celery into 2 inch (5cm) sticks. Cut the cucumber into 2 inch (5cm) lengths, then cut lengthwise into quarters and cut away the seeds to make 'boats'.
2. Blend together the cheese, Pernod, herbs, salt and pepper. Place in a piping bag with a small plain tube and stuff the vegetables. Arrange on a large serving platter.

Serves 6–8

Crab Toasts

Preparation time: 10 minutes, plus chilling time

8oz (250g) crab meat, brown and
    white or mixed
1 tablespoon lemon juice
2oz (50g) butter, melted

1 tablespoon Pernod
salt and pepper
6–8 thin slices wholemeal bread

Crab toasts are a good standby for unexpected guests. Keep a can of crab meat in the cupboard, or use frozen mixed crab meat.

1. Place the crab and lemon juice in a blender or food processor and blend until fairly smooth. Add the butter, Pernod, salt and pepper and mix briefly. Turn into a small dish and smooth the top. Chill until firm (at least 30 minutes).
2. Toast the bread lightly, remove the crusts and cut each slice into nine squares, or cut into fancy shapes with a cutter. Spread with the crab mixture and serve.

Serves 6–8

Pernod Cocktails

PINK PANTHER

2 parts Pernod
1 dash grenadine
4 parts soda
lots of ice

MONKEY GLAND

1 part gin
1 part Pernod
4 parts orange juice
lots of ice

BLUE LAGOON

1 part Pernod
1 part blue curaçao
4 parts lemonade
lots of ice

PERNOD FIZZ

1 part Pernod
5 parts champagne
lots of ice

VAMPIRE

1 part Pernod
1 part Dubonnet
4 parts lemonade
lots of ice

BLACK ORCHID

1 part Pernod
½ part Cointreau
1 part blackcurrant
4 parts lemonade
lots of ice

PERNOD ICEBERG

1 part Pernod
dash of crème de menthe
4 parts tonic
lots of ice

DUMB BLONDE

1 part Pernod
1 part advocaat
4 parts tonic
lots of ice

JELLY BEAN

1 part Pernod
1 part vodka
1 part blackcurrant
4 parts lemonade
lots of ice

PERNOD LASER

1 part Pernod
1 part white rum
3 parts orange juice
dash of grenadine
lots of ice

Pernod is intended to be mixed in the ratio of five parts iced water to one part Pernod. In Scotland, however, it is immensely popular with lemonade, probably because lemonade is traditionally free in Scottish bars.

Neat Pernod is a clear, pale green colour until water is added, when it turns milky. This accounts for the apt nickname used by French workmen – *lait de tigre* – 'tiger's milk'. In café society, it was known as *la fée verte* – 'the green fairy'.

Index